Simon's Pieman

Naomi Thornton
and André Amstutz

GRAFTON BOOKS

A Division of the Collins Publishing Group

LONDON GLASGOW
TORONTO SYDNEY AUCKLAND

Help Your Child To Write

All children love scribbling; turning scribbling into writing is easier than you think. These books will help you to help your child to write. Each one teaches a specific group of letters but you don't need to buy them all. The whole alphabet and practice patterns are printed at the end of all of them.

At first it is best to enjoy the stories and the pictures for themselves. Then, when the child knows the stories, you can use the characters and events to help him learn to write.

Here are some tips:
1. Have ready lots of paper (the books are not for writing in) and any kind of pencil, pen, felt-tip or crayon.
2. Only practise writing skills when your child is relaxed and in the mood. Respond to his need to learn, not your urge to teach.
3. Holding the pencil correctly like the child in the picture is a first step. Reverse the picture for a left-handed child.
4. All the books start with patterns. These are merely 'rhythmic scribbles' to be repeated until the child can draw them with ease. Each one gives practice in the movements needed for certain letters.

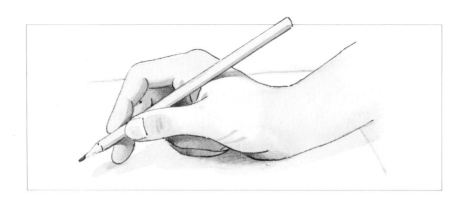

5. It is better for the child to repeat the patterns freely in his own style than to reproduce them accurately but unnaturally.
6. Don't worry about speed. The child will learn best at his own pace.
7. Watching you enjoy the patterns and letters he makes will be more fun for the child than working alone.
8. Remember, there's no need for paper. You can draw letters in the air, in the dust on the sideboard, in sand or on steamed-up windows.
9. When your child knows some letters, help him to use them. When he names an object, get him to write its name down. Get him to label his dog, his bed, his brother, his cup, his jumper. You name it, he can write it. And he'll have fun doing so.

Who is this?

It's Simple Simon going to the fair

Draw the bus stop like this:

Draw the candy sticks like this:

Draw the streamers like this:

Simple Simon met a pieman
Going to the fair
Said Simple Simon to the pieman
Let me taste your ware

A steak and kidney pie please

Draw the pies like this:

To Simple Simon said the pieman
I'm going to the fair
If you want to buy a pie
You'll have to get one there

Said Simple Simon to the pieman
That simply isn't fair
I've only got pie money
I can't afford the fare

Write **p** for pie like this:

p   p   p   p   p   p

Write **s** for steak-and-kidney like this:

s   s   s   s   s

To Simple Simon said the pieman
Just jump aboard the bus
I'll buy your ticket and your pie
So let's not have a fuss

Write **t** for ticket like this:

t t t t t

Write **b** for bus like this:

So Simple Simon ate his pie
And drove the dodgem cars
He rode the roller coaster
And a spaceship to the stars

Write **d** for dodgems like this:

Write **r** for roller coaster like this:

Simple Simon won a fish
But used up all his money

Write **f** for fish like this:

f f f f f f

Soon night came and he was lost –
It wasn't very funny!

Simple Simon met the pieman
Coming from the fair
I'm lost, he cried, so far from home
Please will you take me there

Write **h** for home like this:

h h h h h h

To Simple Simon said the pieman
Here's the bus! Don't cry

I'll swop this ticket for your fish —
And bake it in a pie!

goldfish pie

Write **fish pie**
like this:

fish pie

Now look at the other letters
of the alphabet, on the next page

Practise the patterns, letters and numbers

Grafton Books
A Division of the Collins Publishing Group
8 Grafton Street, London W1X 3LA

Published by Grafton Books 1986
Copyright © André Amstutz 1986

British Library Cataloguing in Publication Data
Thornton, Naomi
  Simon's Pieman. – (Help Your Child To Write; 1)
  1. English language – Alphabet – Juvenile
literature.
  I. Title   II. Amstutz, André   III. Series
  421'.1   PE1155
  ISBN 0-246-12937-9 (Hardback)
  ISBN 0-583-30994-1 (Paperback)

Printed in Spain by Graficas Reunidas